DIVINE RATIOS

DIVINE RATIOS

POEMS | JACQUELINE OSHEROW

LOUISIANA STATE UNIVERSITY PRESS

BATON ROUGE

Published by Louisiana State University Press
lsupress.org

LSU Press Paperback Original

Designer: Michelle A. Neustrom
Typefaces: Bodoni 72, MillerDisplay

Cover illustration (*top to bottom*): *The Ideal City,* ca. 1480s, Galleria Nazionale
delle Marche, Urbino; *The Ideal City,* ca. 1480–1484, The Walters Art Museum,
Baltimore; *The Ideal City,* ca. 1492, Gemäldegalerie, Berlin.

Cataloging-in-Publication Data are available from the Library of Congress.

ISBN 978-0-8071-7771-6 (pbk.: alk. paper) — ISBN 978-0-8071-7974-1 (pdf) —
ISBN 978-0-8071-7973-4 (epub)

for Magda, Dora, Mollie, and Ray

CONTENTS

III

IV

ACKNOWLEDGMENTS

Many thanks to the Jentel Artists' Residency, the Virginia Center for Creative Arts, Las Obras, Portugal, as well as the University of Utah's Taft-Nicholson Center, where many of these poems were begun. Special thanks, too, to the University of Utah Research Committee, which sent me both to Berlin and to China. Many thanks to the Academy of American Poets, for commissioning the poem that became "Inspiration Point, Bryce Canyon, Utah" for its *Imagine Our Parks with Poems* project, to *New Voices* for commissioning "SS Photo, Auschwitz, 1944," and to the editors who published a number of the poems in this book: *Agni:* "Camouflage"; *Antioch Review:* "Views of Ideal Cities: Urbino, Baltimore, Berlin"; *Harvard Review:* "Fast Track: Beijing, Montana, Harlem"; *Image:* "Santo Spirito (Autobiography with Doves)," "x. Benozzo Gozzoli at the Fahai Temple Murals," and "xv. English Library, Ya Li School (Changsha, Hunan Province)"; *Ocean State Review:* "City Dreams: After Bodys Isek Kingelez" and "Psalm 137, Berlin"; *Poetry International:* "Art Deco Sonnet," "Ghazal Season," "ii. At Yueyang Tower," and "v. The Orchid Pavilion Gathering (353 C.E.)"; *Poem-a-Day*, Academy of American Poets: "xiii. Return to Suzhou: Master of the Nets"; *Southern Review:* "iii. Notes from the Exhibit *Streams and Mountains without End*," "vii. Propaganda Museum, Shanghai," "xii. Great Wall," and "xiv. Marco Polo in the Temple of Heaven"; *Tikkun:* "Stumble Stone"; and *32 Poems:* "vi. Datong (Yugong Grottoes)," "xi. Shanghai Taxi," and "xvi. Epilogue: Back Home." Finally, enormous thanks to Wayne Koestenbaum and Barry Weller, who gave such close and valuable attention to this manuscript.

I

Inspiration Point, Bryce Canyon, Utah

Maybe it was just for this that God
pulled water from dry land: to rescue hoodoo
after hoodoo. That's what they're called—

a bastardization of *voodoo*—
these unrepeatable needles of rock,
geology's answer to flakes of snow.

A sound enough hypothesis: dark magic.
But I like God's approach—so straightforward:
the light, the land, the sky, each feat of handiwork

a matter of a single uttered word
(that's the first version; the clumsy second
was more hands-on, with dust and ribs required)

though it's a stretch to claim this place was planned.
Maybe, just like us, God was stupefied;
He rarely knew how any day would end,

had to see things finished to call them *good*.
Here, He might even have done without
the bric-a-brac of the days that followed

except the fourth day's (bodies of light)
essential for the colors of the stone,
the *greater light* especially adroit.

Just watch it nurse a puny flame at dawn—
purple with an edging of vermilion—
by sunrise to a full-fledged conflagration

———

then temper it to golden-rose by noon,
darker still as day begins to fail.
The oranges go bronze, the reds, maroon,

the whole place solid indigo by nightfall,
except on nights when a full or near-full moon
applies its inlay—mother-of-pearl

on a lamina of coral and carnelian—
or the moon's a no-show, no stone visible,
just black on black, spikes and spires gone.

That's when you look up: the sky's Grand Central
(no light pollution; no clouds; conditions ideal),
rush hour's hubbub irresistible,

the stars its thronged commuters, cheek by jowl.
The Park has telescopes (I once saw Jupiter)
but I prefer an open free-for-all,

the peripheral inkling of a meteor
(or was that a satellite?) or diving owl.
Some flora and fauna *did* make their way here

eventually, swashbucklers all:
rattlesnake, manzanita, prickly pear,
its shock of blossoms at the end of April

slow-motion fireworks, the canyon floor
lost beneath magentas, yellows, reds
or bristle-cone pine, launching spectacular

high-wire acrobatics off the cliff sides,
where that gifted horticulturist,
the nuthatch, a glutton for its seeds,

disseminates them when it stops to rest—
quite ingenious of God, if oddly fanciful
for so inveterate a fatalist,

that is, if God's mixed up in this at all.
The Park prefers the Piutes' explanation:
the hoodoos were once the *legend people,*

shape-shifters, native to this region,
turned for some unnamable transgression
by vigilant Coyote into stone,

their face paint still intact, their tradition
of shape-shifting now upheld in unison,
a nonstop frenzy of dissimulation:

now a storm-tossed, now a tranquil, ocean
flocked by scarlet ibis, pink flamingos,
now dreamscape, now valley of the moon,

now ransacked cathedrals' lost rose windows,
now an amphitheater's hushed proscenium,
now leafless aspens, elms, catalpas, willows,

now phantom hollyhock, delphinium,
now flashback, now panicked premonition,
now truce, now skirmish, now pandemonium,

now parachutes (a daredevil battalion
floating toward an ill-fated attack),
now blushing debutantes (their first cotillion),

now parched oasis, now bivouac,
close by each golden tent a golden torch,
now red-robed Russian choirs, now ecstatic

ovations from thick stands of golden birch,
now burnished temple, now tarnished city,
now bands of acolytes—in mosque, in church

or here, assembling legends of Coyote—
scrambling to get down on their untried knees
and thank someone—anyone—for all this beauty,

though maybe it's the frost they ought to praise,
the real creator, according to science:
how it would melt and freeze, melt and freeze

and then, in a matter of mere eons
(no wind involved, windy as it is),
chisel what must be earth's most flimsy stone—

limestone, siltstone, mudstone—into this.
Not surprising, really, when you think what frost
can achieve, in seconds, on a pane of glass—

always a revelation, when a miniaturist
takes his genius for precision large-scale:
the landscape behind the Mystic Lamb as Christ

in the Ghent altarpiece, for example,
an exhaustive primer of floral specimens,
rendered in botanical detail,

art both mainstay and intimate of science—
think Leonardo—and science of art.
What fools we were to leave the Renaissance

behind us, to tear ourselves apart
into more and more obscure specialization.
Not that it matters here. Science and art,

even in conjunction with their on-again
off-again confederate, religion,
are speechless in the presence of this canyon.

Even God needs two versions of Creation
at the start of Genesis. Some things defy
a single overarching explanation.

Maybe everything does, if you look carefully.
And what's a day exactly, when the sun
hasn't yet been added to the sky?

That third day might still be going on,
everything I'm staring at still raw,
God on overdrive, the frost a madman,

consumed by each imaginary flaw.
Am I a witness? an alibi? a spy?
And what's this delirium? this terror? this awe?

Is the sky hallucinating? Am I?
Inspiration Point, Bryce Canyon, Utah
Just let me stand here with an open eye.

Camouflage

An abandoned feather: a dried-out leaf;
a branch: a shed antler; a toad: a stone;
in the high tawny grass a tawny bas-relief
of half-hidden pronghorns on the run;
geese overhead: gridlocked drivers, close,
leaning on their horns; thunder: a truck
barreling down my street, rattling windows
(an enormous semi, when the earthquake struck).
A branchless tree trunk is an obelisk
until its top lifts off, flaps hulking wings
and glides: a great horned owl prowling at dusk.
Soon, perhaps we'll learn—a cricket sings
or is that just evening's quickening pulse?—
to rise and reappear as something else.

Fast Track: Beijing, Montana, Harlem

The Beijing Train Station—my daughter says on Skype—
is a madhouse on a Monday at three a.m.
But I, in the thrall of hawks and antelope,

the closest thing Montana has to mayhem
unless you count the thunder two nights back,
think nothing of it, until, in Harlem,

awake, thanks to an ear-splitting trash truck,
I remember what she said and think again,
unable to conjure up a single flock

of dervish swallows, one sandhill crane
emptying a meadow with its call.
Even the misty valley floor at dawn

seems, from this vantage, hypothetical,
diminished to an image on a screen—
when its abiding genius is its scale.

Is it my failure of imagination
or simply that the human brain can't hold
this much competing information?

fallout from our newly puny world—
Montana giving way to Harlem too fast,
with nothing much to intervene but cloud.

But I also thrill to these absurdly paced—
if not quite majestic—spectacles,
each subway ride an urban vision-quest:

faces, hairdos, fabrics, stiletto heels,
fingers wielding eyeliners and lipsticks
without a smudge to their resplendent nails,

tee-shirts hailing teams or schools or wisecracks
on kick-ass kids who fly in out of nowhere—
the poles makeshift trapezes—nail their tricks,

pass the hat, then move to the next car,
leaving me to translate ads, nostalgic
for *las cucarachas entran pero no pueden salir*

which any passenger from eighties New York
will be able to rattle off forever.
There's even wildlife: rats on the track,

cousins of Montana's muskrat, beaver,
while, above, the newest feral pioneer
is the West's own (a Twitter observer

claims he saw one in a rooftop bar)
supremely adaptable coyote.
Still, no more adaptable than we are,

thirty-eight million of us in a single city,
to get back to my daughter in Beijing
and the dizzying wages of velocity.

But what's diminishing as we're enlarging
our field of vision—what's the toll
(there always is one) we're not acknowledging?

And what's the payoff beyond a jumble
of muddled images we can't quite see
(if we manage to keep hold of them at all)

much less reliably identify?
It's a futile business, accumulation,
thwarted not so much by failing memory

as by a chronic parsimony of attention.
Too late, I realize (I've just turned sixty)
the way I've shortchanged every place I've been;

how a single-minded appetite for novelty
makes every panorama interchangeable,
distinction a finer point of subtlety,

and subtlety, of change so gradual
we're likely to mistake it for duration.
It turns out, I've been insatiable

for precisely the wrong thing. Look at Dickinson,
finite infinity a single room.
Maybe moving around is a distraction,

though I'm not quite sure I can say what from.
My daughter's in China. I'll have to go there.
And another of my daughters lives in Harlem.

But what a pity I never stay longer
in a single spot—any would do,
since, once your gaze begins to linger,

snatches of transcendence glimmer through
even the least welcoming surface;
and there are furtive gems in every view

to which only patience offers access.
That valley in Montana, for example,
always willing, at an instant's notice,

to flaunt its sage, lupine, cattail, thistle,
flash a broadtail hummingbird or two,
throw in, perhaps, a bonus hawk and kestrel

locked in their lopsided pas-de-deux,
a moose chomping willows in the wetlands . . .
Who knows what grace it's keeping incognito?

Here too (I've moved again; I'm on Greyhound's
Philadelphia Express, a triumvirate
of smokestacks on my left) the Meadowlands

distract me with two herons and an egret
from undetected secrets on my right.
Still, I couldn't say I wholly regret

my rapid-fire pace, however profligate
with unseen wonders. The overstuffed
(from Art Nouveau to Byron to George Eliot)

my go-to habitat—I love a spendthrift,
Bauhaus a chilly afterthought, haiku
for all its nimbleness, a tad bereft

of syllables for my taste, though I do
wish I hadn't missed more than I've seen;
but I'd miss something in every view.

Maybe we all do. Doesn't Dickinson
ignore her—albeit modest—mountain
to focus on its *little gentian?*

Maybe that's the trick: to focus in—
even the minuscule rewards attention—
or better still, to find a way to listen;

everything has truths it could pass on,
each with its own compelling entourage
of likeness and divergence and suggestion

waiting for their instant on a page.
It's too late—sixty!—to indulge them all,
but surely I could hit a higher percentage?

Do I keep moving? or at last stand still?
Either way, it's doubtful I'll find refuge
(is that what I'm after?) from the exile

I'm only just beginning to acknowledge.
But from which Eden? When did I fall?
Or is this what people mean by pilgrimage?

each stop along the way an oblique peephole
onto an interior mirage,
as if all landscape had an inner double,

its buried coordinates always on the verge
of revealing themselves once and for all:
phantom wetlands, alive with plumage;

a dreamscape subway's nonstop spectacle;
a prime, untrammeled swath of acreage
still echoing a sandhill crane's shrill call

through fields of lupine, cattail, thistle, sage
rendered, by a rising mist, invisible
so all you see is space itself writ large
even as what marks it out grows small.

II

PUTTING A QUESTION
TO THE SPRING

i. Suzhou Garden, February

In the Putting a Question to the Spring Pavilion
I put a question to the spring.
She answers *plum blossom, bamboo, pine.*

To me it's a fairly burning question:
how do you bear it all winter long?
But the Putting a Question to the Spring Pavilion

simply redirects my line of vision
outward, past its eaves, toward a flourishing
of plum blossom, bamboo and pine

the *three friends of winter* (or so they're known
in ancient poems, paintings). February's beginning
but near the Putting a Question to the Spring Pavilion:

clustered needles, daggers, green on green
and petals on spare gray branches opening
(plum blossom, bamboo and pine).

Could I survive a bitter season?
What three friends would blunt its sting?
I put questions to the spring in her pavilion;
she asks the plum blossom, bamboo, pine.

ii. At Yueyang Tower

Water sky
one color
My daughter tries to translate on the fly.

She says the poem's by Li Bai.
Eight characters. She makes out four:
water sky

one color. What might the other four words be?
We've made a pilgrimage to Yueyang Tower;
my daughter tries to translate on the fly.

Poor Du Fu has to hold the rail and cry
in his "Climbing Yueyang Tower"
(it too has water and sky;

he's on a boat *old* and *ill* and *lonely*).
I never find the poem—did she mistake the author?—
my daughter tries to translate on the fly.

Still, except for a cement barge, behind me
lake and sky are one consistent silver.
My daughter tries to translate on the fly:
one color water sky

---

iii. Notes from the Exhibit
Streams and Mountains without End

(The Metropolitan Museum of Art, December 2017)

I took copious notes, but I can't read them
except Sima Huai's twelfth-century quotation
Now Duanheng has written a soundless poem.

Which scroll was it? I forget each painter's name.
So many details clamoring for attention:
tiny people, houses, trees . . . I like to read them

by moving alongside them over time,
each a sort of leisurely narration.
Now Duanheng has written a soundless poem.

Does he mean brush strokes? The Chinese delirium
for the fleeting discipline of ink in motion?
(I distinguish *grass, running, seal* but I can't read them.)

Or would he strip down every known artistic medium
to a single knife-edge of revelation?
O Sima Huai, send me a poem

that can commandeer an eye across a room.
Even the people in the scroll will listen.
Their lips are moving. Can you read them?
They're reciting Duanheng's soundless poem.

iv. Reading Bai Juyi (772–846) atop Lu Shan

This June, across the world, all petals have fallen
I so regretted the loss of spring
(At the site of Dalin Temple, atop Lu Shan,

I find Bai Juyi's poem on a sign)
But here, the peach blossom is just beginning
The diminished world, its petals fallen,

now blurred as mist spirals up the mountain,
might have been what set the poet climbing,
Dalin Temple, atop Lu Shan,

so high, so old, so curative a shrine,
Mao used its site for a decisive gathering
(new blooms begun, old petals fallen).

Perhaps Mao came at Bai Juyi's suggestion,
the promise of a second chance at spring.
All the poet had to do was climb Lu Shan:

no autumn, no winter, no fallow season.
I'd envy him, my losses less forgiving
than those blossoms refound atop Lu Shan,
but June's long past; his petals, too, have fallen.

v. The Orchid Pavilion Gathering, 353 CE

A wine cup in *a swirling, splashing stream*
(poets along both banks, the Orchid Pavilion).
Whoever it reached would drink and write a poem.

The calligrapher Wang Xizhi recalled this game
in his *Preface from the Orchid Pavilion*
(*lofty peaks, luxuriant trees, the swirling stream*).

It was buried with an emperor in his tomb.
We only have copies, but they, too, stun
with the ever-out-of-reach, the waylaid poem

escaped as brushstroke, ideogram.
Scroll after scroll depicts the scene:
drunken poets sprawled along the stream

each waiting for the cup to come to him,
some greedily and some in desperation.
Who is ever sure to reach a poem?

When future generations recall my time
they'll feel what I feel about generations gone . . .
A wine cup in *a swirling, splashing stream;*
whoever it reaches drinks and writes a poem.

vi. Datong (Yugong Grottoes)

Overwhelmed, I wonder: can I see this?
The world has turned unreadable, too vast:
cliffs of grottoes carved with giant Buddhas

and their tiny endless entourage (believers,
flora, fauna) hint at all I've missed,
coming, as I have, too late to see this

on its own terms, my useless compass
(Florence, Michelangelo, the west)
has, for grottos carved with giant Buddhas,

no known coordinates. I grasp at likeness;
this curve of vine or antler might have graced
a Romanesque altar. It's how I see this.

Then I learn such sculpture *came* to the Chinese
from India, where Alexander, pressing east,
had introduced it, that giant Buddhas

and Romanesque altars share one source!
The world's small again. We all can see this.
In Umbria right now, a Chinese tourist
finds, on slender crosses, sad gaunt Buddhas.

vii. Propaganda Museum, Shanghai

(After *Experience the Happiness of the Commune*)

For pictures earth, for poems sky,
a worker-painter, and above his head
in spare white lines: a dream of industry

so finely etched, it might be calligraphy,
all white, though his brush is dripping red.
For pictures earth, for poems sky.

Hydropower plants, farm machinery
hover on the blue in wisps, like cloud,
as if the sky itself were dreaming industry.

Soon enough, the dreams will go awry,
but in this one dispatch from the Great Leap Forward
borrowing the blue of the sky

to write poems is revolutionary,
relying on earth to draw pictures (your palette red)
part and parcel of a dream of industry,

a brushstroke's incantatory bull's-eye
entrusted with a world-changing crusade.
In that pristine expanse, who dreamed what industry
would make of earth, poems, pictures, sky?

viii. Second Half, Yueyang Tower

It *was* Li Bai. Later my daughter found it:
Water sky one color
Wind moon no limit.

Her translation, she explains, is approximate,
the poem's treasure
(too late for me to find it)

both hidden and revealed in the Chinese, intricate
with verbal pairings. *Wind/moon* is *love affair*
or *scenic vista*. As for *no limit*

we can only speculate:
bright, inconstant, glinting in water
and gone just as—too late—we think we've found it.

Unless, as in Hebrew, *wind* means *spirit*
and Li Bai *caught* that moon in the river?
The evidence: *wind moon no limit.*

He died of drink—not drowning—exile, regret,
what he'd sought *sea sky one color*
in his hand *wind moon no limit*
late, too late perhaps, but he had found it.

ix. At the Fahai Temple Murals
(Ming Dynasty, 1439–1443)

Sheer amazement—even in the dark
(we're given flashlights, but they have little power).
I light a bit of wall and look and look.

Our guide's speaking Chinese, so I just gawk,
aim my flashlight randomly and wander
(light harms the fragile paint, that's why it's dark).

I find lotus, peony, clusters of thick
white rhododendron, scholar-tree flower,
identifying species as I look

as if this were a Ming botany textbook.
Meanwhile, her introduction over,
our guide angles her light across the dark,

coaxing—calm, unearthly, beatific—
a dim, exquisite figure to cohere.
Buddha? Bodhisattva? I look and look

but the others in my group begin to arc
their torsos, bow their heads, palms locked in prayer.
What is it they can see? Dare I look?
Or do I just return politely to the dark?

x. Benozzo Gozzoli at the Fahai Temple Murals

Fahai Frescoes, 1439–1443
Benozzo Gozzoli, Capella dei Magi, 1459

How can I not think of Benozzo Gozzoli?
There are elephants, lions, birds, a wolf, a leopard,
lavish costumes, jewels; faith was pageantry

both in Medici Florence and the Ming dynasty,
twenty years and half a planet apart.
Coincidence? Destiny? Benozzo Gozzoli

had Giotto, Fra Angelico, a legacy
one would have thought essential to such art.
But scrolls and painted caves have their own pageantry

and one might get fine gifts (forgive me, magi)
from lords and ladies of the imperial court,
their robes dripping real pearls. Benozzo Gozzoli

adorned *his* splendid cavalcade of magi
with gold and gold brocade, the horses girt
in gilded chains and bridles, pageantry

(along with grace, precision) an unfailing ally
(not to mention excess) of the spirit.
It runs over, transfigures into ecstasy.
O Ming Masters. O Benozzo Gozzoli.

xi. Shanghai Taxi

My daughter teaches us to recite a poem
in Chinese—a poem all schoolchildren learn,
Li Bai: *bright moonlight, frost, missing home.*

It's for the teacher who taught *her* the poem;
we practice in the taxi to the station.
Everyone in China can recite this poem.

Our driver, stunned, joins in, has us mimic him;
slowly, he exaggerates each tone:
Bright moonlight, frost on the ground, missing home.

He laughs and laughs, amused by our game
while I'm trying (impossible) to imagine
all *my* countrymen united by a poem

though, once, a cab driver recited Omar Khayyam
all the way from the Salt Lake Airport in Persian
when I told him what I do (he missed home)

and my father-in-law could reel off every psalm
in Hebrew (a brief shtetl education):
The sun will not smite . . . or the moon . . . help will come . . .
How can we sing God's song away from home?

xii. Great Wall

At first, it's simply part of the terrain
but, all at once, outside our bus's window
the hills unleash their curving spine of stone

and then (we round a bend) a golden dragon
starts slithering our way—steady, slow,
so wholly intimate with the terrain,

every rise or swerve becomes its own.
And there's no end to it—our eyes can follow,
goading the hills, a curving spine of stone

out to the very edge of the horizon,
where, for centuries, through wind and snow,
it's kept its perfect watch on this terrain.

Not that it offered any real protection.
The Mongols conquered anyway, made Beijing *Daidu,*
allowed the hillsides' curving spine of stone

to fall (the Ming repaired it later) into ruin,
for all its builders' drudgery and sorrow,
their own spines long part of this terrain,
every curve of wall an unclaimed headstone.

xiii. Return to Suzhou: Master of the Nets

It was meant to conjure the life of a fisherman—
solitude, simplicity and peace—
hence the name—*Master of the Nets Garden.*

Not the real life, of course, but what a nobleman
(who else would bankroll such quiet grace?)
imagines when he thinks *life of a fisherman:*

the sea in miniature, harnessed, halcyon
abundant fish (giant koi, not bass).
It's a stand-in wilderness, a Chinese garden—

each tree a forest, each rock a mountain—
for those obliged to keep close to the house.
There are even breaking waves: our would-be fisherman

could watch, from covered walkways, a procession
of ripples launched across his fishpond's surface
by pelting raindrops; his master gardener

dispensed perfection even in the rain.
I visit in a downpour—paradise—
while, out on open sea, a master fisherman,
expanse itself his garden, plies his nets.

xiv. Marco Polo in the Temple of Heaven

I love to imagine Marco Polo coming here
though there's no Chinese record of his presence
and so many oddities and wonders never appear

in his *Book of the Marvels of the World,* sceptics conjecture
that he only learned of China trading with Persians
on the Black Sea. Did he even come here?

He used a Persian word in *Book of Marvels* for a feature
unique to Chinese ships—that's their evidence—
and that foot-binding, chopsticks, the Great Wall never appear.

But at the Temple of Heaven, nine circles ring the altar.
Nine circles, as in Dante's heavens,
sufficient proof to me that Marco came here.

How else could Dante have learned heavenly structure?
He was Marco's contemporary, in a next-door province;
He could have met him, stalked him, eavesdropped . . . nine circles appear

in his hell, purgatory *and* heaven. How did they get there?
Or was Dante's pilgrimage real, as he contends?
Was Marco's? Either way, wonders appear.
They're calling even now *come here, come here . . .*

xv. English Library, Ya Li School
(Changsha, Hunan Province)

The Yellow River begins in heaven
a student recites at my daughter's school
its waters run to the sea and never return . . .

I've asked for a poem; she offers this one
in Chinese, then English, her translation simple.
The ancients, she says, *thought rivers began in heaven*

Don't they? But I'm too amazed to listen.
We have the same words, I say, *in our ancient Bible:*
All the rivers run to the sea . . . But ours *return.*

Ecclesiastes, chapter one, verse seven:
All the rivers run to the sea, yet the sea is not full
they return to the place they began. Can he mean *heaven?*

In the meantime, I find *her* poem: Li Bai, drunk again.
Ecclesiastes might just mean nature's cyclical:
There's nothing new under the sun . . . All things return

His solution? *Eat, drink and be merry.* Li Bai's? *more wine*
He's got a *fine horse* and *furs* he's willing to sell . . .
They're locked in a drunken shouting match in heaven
They return . . . they never . . . return . . . never . . . return

xvi. Epilogue, Back Home

I'm left now with the poems, their Chinese
pure after-echo, thunder chasing lightning,
unrelenting pressure, then release.

You have to dream, reading translations. Otherwise
they're closed to you. A bowstring tightening
behind an arrow—that's how I hear Chinese—

and then let fly, all speed and thwack and hiss.
(Did I travel there or just read the writing?)
Unrelenting pressure, then release.

As children, we would count the seconds, freeze,
tensing for the thunder after lightning.
Each second meant a mile, but in Chinese

no time elapses; each tone is endless.
Bai Juyi, Du Fu, Li Bai? They're still writing
(unrelenting pressure, then release)

and I'm still chasing whatever it is
that infiltrates an instant, turns it loose,
with repercussions lasting, spreading, widening

like ripples in a pond (the pond's Chinese).
Unrelenting pressure, then release.

III

Santo Spirito
(Autobiography with Doves)

My visitations come
from herons, egrets,
hummingbirds, in
certain seasons: ram's
horns, bitter herbs
and that winning
combination—citron,
willow, myrtle, palm—
contracted in oak-gall
ink on primed and
sanctioned parchment
in sacred, if much
disputed, words.

I thought the Holy Spirit
was a collar on God
the Father's robes as He
stood—sad, accusing—
over the dying Christ
in that chock-full showpiece,
Santa Maria Novella, my
first time in Florence,
December 1978, Masaccio
a name I'd never heard

and I was so enamored
of the teeming Ghirlandaio,
its faces like the faces
in the dream-inducing streets,
its birds, its clouds, its gilt-
brocaded gowns, its two

intriguing figures
(attributed to Ghirlandaio's
wunderkind apprentice,
Michelangelo) turning
their backs to me
to stare over a wall
at something only
they and he can see,

I barely attended
to the gripping
triple spectacle
unfolding three-
quarters of a
nave away, waiting
for me to rise
to its ethereal
occasion, its respite
from importunate
detail, waiting, even,
for me to misconstrue
its sense entirely—
ridiculous, really,
the thing is called
La Trinità and anyone
can see that that's a dove.

But what did I know
about the Holy Trinity?,
its sole association
the name of a school
near the mostly Jewish
neighborhood where
I grew up, oblivious
to who was meant
by *Father,* who by *Son,*

and fearful at the sound
of *Holy Ghost.*

Even now, I only know
what Masaccio has
told me, aided by his
unassuming dove
and the hopeful
virtuosos who
put brush to still-
wet plaster, bent
on capturing
before it set
that first suspicion
of transfiguration
hanging on an angel's
lightning utterance
or a sprinkling from
John's—*the spirit
descending from heaven
like a dove*—surprisingly
unprepossessing bowl.

I had always imagined
it was Noah's dove returned,
or the dove as beloved
in the clefts of the rock
(an allegory for God,
the rabbis say)
*let me see your countenance,
let me hear your voice*
and here he is emerging
from *the secret places
of the stairs* to purify
a deity's unlikely
bulk or amplify

a bombshell
from an angel . . .

though sometimes
the dove stays
nearly secret,
dissolving—Fra
Lippo Lippi—in a dove-
gray loggia wall, or
disguised as another
line of cirrus cloud
in the sky above Piero's
baptized Christ,
its gliding body
approached straight on,
head downward,
wings outspread—

but the dove's
heralded with
fanfare in Piero's
Annunciation,
trotted out in
quattrocento
neon: swooping
toward Mary,
from just inside
the frame,
ushered in
and trailed
by beaten gold.

And there is no
dove where
Pontormo gets

involved, just
an inside glimpse
of the domestic,
its trompe l'oeil
so convincing, I
myself—intruder?
voyeur?—feel
like I'm a piece
of the tableau:

        Mary,
hand on banister,
foot midstep, swivels
to face backward
as she's gliding
up the stairs, toward
a new and strangely
intimate imperative
reconfiguring the
far-flung syllables
of what remains
to her of her
own name

        coming from
the other side of
an ugly polychrome
altar, added to this
chapel in the eighteenth
century—perhaps
covering over
the missing dove?

or was Pontormo's
instinct just to let

the Holy Spirit
infiltrate his
universe invisibly?

or maybe it's simply
I who cannot see?

In Leonardo's
Annunciation,
is there a dove?
I certainly can't
find one—but
Leonardo *is* famous
for hiding things,
his revelations coherent
only when reflected
in a glass and, even
then, inscrutable
with code, or,

worse, as with
his masterwork,
sabotaged from
within, impermanence
a feature of their very
make-up: encrypted
in an undercoat of
luminous white lead
the promise
of certain dissolution.

Perhaps he was
suspicious of
the actual?
Intolerant of
its inherent

weaknesses? Or
was he merely trying
to counter the affront
of his own (to him
prodigious, however
inaccessible to us)
incapacitating
limitations?

unless it was
a matter of faith?
he didn't believe?

But even Fra Angelico,
devout Dominican,
seems to have perfected
his divine *Annunciation*
without assistance
from any dove.

Still, halfway down
the hallway, above
his freshly baptized
Christ, the dove couldn't
be more conspicuous,
encircled by a halo
of concentric clouds
arranged to channel
never-ending light:
the heavens' makeshift cup
running over into St. John's
bowl, as ripple after ripple
upends the lake of sky
as if the dove were
skipping pebbles
with his wings

or does the dove
itself serve as pebble?
skipped by a, for once,
lighthearted God,
at this, perhaps
the only wholly

jubilant occasion
in His only child's
only earthly life.

I mean, of course, before
the Resurrection.

Forgive me if I'm
getting this entirely
wrong. I'm just
trying to describe
what I can see,
or rather what I've
missed, or perhaps
have not seen yet,
or all of the above
in combination

unless—who knows?
it's been working
on me all along,
its proselytizing
deftly subliminal,

like the edgy
come-ons urban
legend claims
were strategically
concealed in

advertisements:
romance by a lake
or in a sports car
or a yacht and
the word *cancer*
secreted in
the smoke
encircling a just-
lit cigarette.

Though I grew up
on those commercials
and I never smoked.
Maybe we're not so
impressionable.
Maybe we simply are
what we are. And
I—what can I tell
you?—remain a Jew,
born too soon after
the war, no matter
what I look at, what
I see. Some disquiet
can be difficult
to shake; paranoia's
mother's milk to me

and I can still call up
my childhood terror
at the spurting blood
from Jesus after Jesus
after Jesus: those dreaded
rooms in the museum
I could never race through
fast enough, always
catching sight of at least

one Jesus spurting arcs
of blood, caught in
tiny bowls by stoic
angels, unbearable
to a squeamish
child like me

and then, floating
around, that
alarming phrase.
Imagine the havoc
a *Ghost* might inflict
with the fanatic
dispensation of the *Holy*.
And where, exactly,
would this ghost be?
Maybe it was mixed
up with the spurting
blood, for which,
though murky on
precise details, I'd
heard accusations
hurled at me.

If only I had known
that it had wings,
to which, all my life,
I've been susceptible,
dreamily poring
over my *Golden Book
of Birds,* memorizing
names and stunning
features, half of me
dubious I'd ever find
these creatures in

the flesh and half of me
forever on the lookout:

from the cardinals
my mother never
tired of pointing
out, clashing
with the mauve
of our azaleas,

to the hoopoe
I caught sight of
just the other
afternoon in
the ginestra-
perfumed woods
above Assisi,
overdressed
as usual and
showing off
his hard-won
if outlandish
frippery

and just now
there's an egret
out the window
of my train,
preening in
the shallows
of Trasimeno,
entirely indifferent
to his passing
devotee, as
my lethargic

carriage hugs
his shore.

Maybe each one
is a holy spirit?
or maybe, once
again, I've entirely
missed the point,
off-kilter as I
am in the face
of holiness
as something
human beings
are meant to see

which is why—
as soon as my
train arrives
in Florence—I
head for the façade
of Santo Spirito
left empty now
half a millennium
though Brunelleschi
drafted a design,

its blank, blank
frontispiece an
oddball shape
fit for an ascetic's
wedding cake
(a tiered lapsed triangle
with flourishes draped
as if to camouflage
its bungled edges)
or regalia for

an earthbound
fledgling angel,
with triple sets of
unavailing wings,

its high rose
window, a plain
circle on the outside,
commandeering
as a Cyclops' eye,
and its three forbidding
rectangles—the central
one immense—suggestive
more of barriers
than entrances
though I've come
through them
dozens of times.

It's a miracle
of grace when you
walk in, a rare
Florence church
requiring no ticket
for admission, but
I, resolute, remain
outside, to let my
eyes adjust—after
weeks of masterpiece—
to the even-handed
discipline of blankness

despite the doves
shot through with light
in the sacristy's stained-
glass lunettes, the high-

glazed doves in terracotta,
white on their medallions'
trademark blue, the meek,
leaden dove in the pietra
serena floor, most likely
hidden by a passing shoe.

I'm not inside, I'm
out here, staring and
staring at this vacant wall
the color of uninterrupted
parchment, gradually
yielding up its pale
expanse, as if it were
unrolling its own scroll
almost translucent in
the waning light, primed
until its surface mimics pearl

perhaps in preparation
for a pious scribe, who'll
immerse his body in
the ritual bath, stir
his ink, sharpen his quill
and stay the emptiness
with thick black strokes
and a binding admixture
of miracle:

a universe from
utterance, a likeness
blessed, good and evil
dangling from a tree,
a dove returning
to solid land, solid
land emerging from

the sea, a voice
in flames at last
acknowledging itself
I will be what I will be

but I'm ahead of myself,
not ready for this yet,
unwilling to give up
this supple blankness
wide-open, burning,
immaculate, this infinite
façade of Santo Spirito,
indulging pilgrims, sinners,
random guests, gorging
us on everything we've
yearned to see, pledging
each petitioner a *yes*

yes to the dove,
yes to the Holy Spirit,
yes to their sublime apologists
yes to yet another deafening transcription
from the red-hot Hebrew alphabet,
yes to the possible,
the unattainable, the precise,
yes to the wholly inaccurate,
yes to grace, *yes* to vision,
but not yet, not quite yet.

Ghazal Season

Outside it's gold again. My ghazal season.
Once, I wrote a ghazal trimmed in gold,

to mirror the implausible transfusion
of waning light to leaf, itself a gold-

inflected mirror, chlorophyll and sun
distilled to pure reflection, gold to gold

to gold, reflected and distilled again.
As if possessed, I siphoned bits of gold

(revising as I traveled through Siena)
from Madonnas' haloes (even the gold

around their harrowed faces doleful, stricken)
and repurposed them as blazing cottonwood,

transfigured linden, willow, golden aspen.
I too was grieving. My father was dead

after a long and grueling mental decline
and my ex-husband (in memory: gold

before psychosis and its brutal haul set in)
had left embers in his wood stove still gold

and slept as they rekindled. His house burned.
(Smoke inhalation. Fifty-four years old.)

Their voices haunt my ghazal—incantation
both painful and consoling—like this gold,

auguring, as it does, a cruel horizon
even as it dazzles. Perhaps all gold

is trailed by sorrow, all benediction,
protection and foreboding intermingled.

In the museum—jewel of jewels—I roamed alone,
compounding each Madonna's store of gold,

her grief, her solace, her rare compassion
with half-formed couplets, finished in gold,

winding and rewinding through my head.
Madonnas. Rhymes. Refrains. An aural vision.

Don't grieve Jackie don't grieve the voices said.
But how can I not grieve? It's ghazal season.

Art Deco Sonnet

(In South Beach, Remembering the Tyson)

O dream palaces of my mother's childhood—
O sleekness, O pizzazz, O mirrors, O chrome,
O remnant inklings of a light-struck world
that deemed a moving picture an occasion
(O Gable, Harlow, Harpo, Garbo, Bogart)
for sculpture, frieze, mosaic, mohair velvet,
carpets lush with fronds—royal palm or fern,
somewhat worse for wear by the time we'd tread them,
my sister and I, to bask in Day and Hudson
with our shared Night 'n Day or Baby Ruth.
When it closed, Mirow's Furs bought the Tyson,
put a mink-clad mannequin in the ticket booth,
restored the murals, fixtures, sleek décor
now long since gutted for an outlet store.

City Dreams: After Bodys Isek Kingelez

(The Museum of Modern Art, December, 2018)

Cities made of toothpaste boxes, matchsticks,
tinfoil, coke cans, wrapping paper, light,
cardboard, cigarette packs (Camels), thumbtacks,

their moxie: whimsy, razzle-dazzle, delight.
One building's a carousel, one's a shark fin,
a cash register, a thurible, a bat

napping upside down, microscope, fan,
the do-it-yourself frippery my Tinkertoys
once coveted (I always let them down),

phantasmagoric as Flushing Meadows
in nineteen-sixty-four—the New York World's Fair—
but without the commotion, crowds and noise,

or even laws of physics (in miniature
they seem a good deal easier to bypass).
Don't mistake me. That New York World's Fair

was full-blown exaltation, sleek with promise
of a future all machinery and ease
to a greedy eight-year-old with open eyes

and I'm there again, thanks to Kingelez
I am artist, sculptor, designer, engineer. . . .
He too believed *no one had a vision like this*

since time immemorial he could shape the future.
No doubt, a dreamer had to be outrageous
in Belgian Congo, then Republic of Congo, Zaire,

Democratic Republic of Congo, a place
condemned to civil war in perpetuity
(it's raging now), to me synonymous

with ongoing horror and atrocity.
And here's Kingelez, injecting whimsy
into dream city after dream city,

each a fleeting detour, however flimsy
(chocolate boxes, face-cream boxes, bottlecaps)
around empire's relentless legacy:

scorched villages, disease, dictatorships
(the only news we hear on the rare occasions
when the Congo's mentioned) child soldiers, rapes . . .

For a child, says UNICEF, seeking donations,
the DRC is *the world's most dangerous place.*
How, then, did it give birth to concoctions

whose abiding spirit is playfulness?
Where did it come from, this joy incarnate?
How did Kingelez get to be Kingelez?

It's never quite explained in the exhibit,
not even the accompanying video,
which offers glimpses of the rundown street

on which he lived and worked—the street's his studio—
and then gives a quick tour of Kinshasa,
stopping for a close look at the statue

of *héro national,* Patrice Lumumba,
also resolute, hand in the air,
condemned for dreaming of uniting Africa

and now so safely dead they've named a square
for him in Brussels, though his firing squad
had orders from Belgium. Behind him, a tower

meant as his memorial, still uncompleted,
does its best to keep Kinshasa's sky,
with its golden needle, inoculated

or perhaps sedated or, simply, high.
For Kingelez, it was clearly a prototype;
he has a tower just this shape, piercing *his* sky.

Is it a message? A strategy to keep
Lumumba's untried memory alive?
An accusation? A promise? A hope?

Maybe—had Lumumba managed to live—
these dreaming cities might be life-size,
in a bustling Congo where children thrive.

Not likely, but I can still feast my eyes
here, at this safe distance, in MoMA
despite a lifetime of obliviousness

(on a map, could I even locate Kinshasa?)
to the news from Congo. At the moment:
forced closings, due to attacks, of ebola

clinics, though the disease is rampant.
In other words, crisis upon crisis.
Surely people in a country as deficient

in most of living's bare necessities
as—by all accounts—Kingelez' homeland
should at least be allowed to fantasize?

And why should fantasy be constrained
to ceasefire, health, equilibrium?
Still, how astonishing to find

myself in a Congolese man's dream,
I, who've barely witnessed deprivation,
much less endured it, roam his *Ville Fantôme*

past zany structures: a pirate's galleon,
a carafe, a luna moth, a rooster's crest,
until I'm back at the GE pavilion

believing everything I'm being promised
The Magic Skyway   Futurama   ogling marvels,
now gliding, steered by Pepsi-Cola, past

an archipelago of singing dolls
(is there one from Congo?)   *Progressland*
now envying the girl who gets to speak on Bell's

picture telephone to a girl in Disneyland.
She's forgotten in the whirr of IBM—
the *Information Machine,* a sensory whirlwind

in a spaceship/theater that starts to climb
then beams the wizardry of the computer
on nine different screens at the same time,

all this with the blessing of the Unisphere—
twelve stories of steel! It triumphs, preens,
so invincible, it keeps on standing there,

the fair's last remnant, lording over Queens,
anomalous now, if brash, cocksure,
and doleful, stoical, as if it mourns

the dazzling, still undelivered future
I avidly embraced without a question,
the lucky fallout from the lucky star

beneath which I was born, my lucky nation
(that is, for my kind), prosperity
in its very air, or at least on every station

(there were four) on our black-and-white TV,
so full-to-bursting with boundless progress
I pitied everyone who'd lived before me.

Meanwhile, in the Congo, my CIA
was propping up a man their own website
(in a just declassified dossier)

describes as a *reviled kleptocrat,*
Mobutu—our *best . . . friend on the continent,*
who drove his country (let me quote

in full the analyst's concluding comment)
into economic ruin and ultimately
political chaos. His government

remained in power a third of a century,
thanks almost entirely to us.
And I only come to know this history

because I fell in love with some dream cities
and wanted to understand their source,
how a man—Bodys Isek Kingelez—

born into such a different universe
had conjured up my own lost dreams in his.
Of course, we did spend nearly sixty years

on the same planet, lopsided though it is.
Perhaps there's no surprise then; maybe dream
is our ideal—our only?—meeting place;

at least it's free of any pressing problem.
(More ebola dead in the eastern Congo
just this morning and no way to bury them.)

As for Kingelez, what did he know?
He was jubilant, his country independent;
who could tell how far its dreams might go?

Things are rarely clear in their own moment,
and, after time, they're often less so—
yet another compelling argument

(though it won't help the ailing Congo
or the other countries, ad infinitum
where we've propped up leaders like Mobutu,

now, even our own) to succumb to dream—
which is what, forgive me, I'm about to do—
to the wanderer, adrift in a museum,

listless, at loose ends, incognito
even to herself, suddenly found
in a full-on, face-to-face rendezvous

with the future she'd long ago abandoned,
amazingly intact (could it have been there
all along? or has it just returned,

the last fifty-five years a blink, a blur?),
stunned to find the child it left behind—
what had parted them?—still dreaming there,

its proselyte, still loyal, spellbound,
either delusional or unaware
of nonstop rumblings along the near
bereft horizon or just beyond.

IV

Views of Ideal Cities:
Urbino, Baltimore, Berlin

Maybe it's overkill, the *Ideal City*
in the ducal palace of Urbino:
an ideal painting of an ideal city
in an ideal palace on a hill
gold- or rose-tinged (depending on the light)
with the ideal domes and towers
of ideal Urbino—the very city
for which the painting was commissioned
along with two others now far-flung—
by the legendary Federico
da Montefeltro—whose jagged profile
in a knock-out portrait by Piero
still bedazzles crowds in the Uffizi—
a duke reputed to have wandered
incognito through Urbino's streets
to monitor the welfare of his citizens,
so steeped in Humanist munificence
he even granted equal status to
the Jews, Urbino so empathically
ideal both in substance and in form
I confuse it in my memory with
the painting,

    especially as both
appear to inhabit three dimensions,
the painting a hymn to rediscovered
gods of mathematics and their sublime
new-fangled stratagem: perspective,
as if the Renaissance were a question
of impeccable proportion, divine
ratios like those Pythagoras
surmised into a music of the spheres,

the work of architecture: listening in,
arresting the harmonies in travertine
and brick, with a predatory eye on Greece
and Rome,

                whose influence is even greater
on the panel purchased with the contents
of a Papal envoy's Roman palazzo
by a wheeler-dealer railway magnate
from Baltimore—where it's still on display
in the museum that bears his name, homage
to Rome in every feature of the painting:
an airier construction of the Arch
of Constantine; a precise, if dainty,
Coliseum; even the octagon
modeled on the Florence baptistery
(which legend mistakenly established
on the ruins of a Roman Temple)
was thought to be a loving nod to Rome,
as is the statuary of the virtues,
studied by the panels' only visible
inhabitants: Justice, Fortitude,
Moderation and Baltimore's own
unexpected modus operandi:
Magnanimity, so buoying
to me one oppressive June afternoon
in a stifling Bolton Hill laundromat,
I'm ashamed I've taken so long to pay
it homage: there I was, at a complete
loss—when had I last used a laundromat?—
with endless loads of my graduating
daughter's weeks? months? of neglected laundry
and before I even managed to ask
my inevitable bumbling questions,
these patient women, likely in that place
week in, week out, were showing me the ropes

(where to put my quarters, laundry, soap),
finding me a basket, a plastic chair.
They'd apologize for interrupting
(I was reading a book) *excuse me ma'am*
when a better machine (not that I could
tell the difference) became available
or a cycle I'd put in motion was done.
How it's stayed with me, that gratuitous
collective kindness, the defeated face
of my supermarket benefactor
telling me to come back the next day—
we get deliveries in the morning;
come at nine; I'll save you some—after
searching high and low for cardboard boxes,
Baltimore a model ideal city,
if not what our painter had in mind,
the reflex benevolence on those squat
red-brick streets perhaps set in motion on
a grade-school trip—it's not impossible—
by the civic-minded duke's noble panel,
his principles perhaps attributed
to the elaborate capital nearby
its contours also borrowed from Greece and Rome.

For years, I knew the third *Ideal City*
only from a poster I lugged around
half of Italy in a plastic tube,
then wedged slantwise into overhead bins
on my multiple stopovers from Rome
Vedute delle Città Ideale.
All three panels, one atop the other,
in my dining room a quarter century,
so out of date, the attribution reads
scuola di Piero della Francesca
(now each painting bears its painter's name).

And though it's written (if in tiny print)
beneath the third *veduta* on the poster,
I'd completely forgotten where it hangs,
forgotten its existence as a self-
sufficient painting, until seventy-
one years after the end of World War II
and fifty or so past a childhood
imbued with tales and photos of its horrors
I decided it was time to face Berlin

about which I knew absolutely nothing
beyond its not distant enough past,
not even the name of the Gemälde-
galerie, much less that the first painting
on display in its Italian wing
would be my unwitnessed *Ideal City*,
a shock to my system, more far-reaching
than the two I'd seen, evocative
with only now accessible detail:
a tiny laurel glimpsed above a wall
through an arched doorway beneath a loggia,
sails of tiny sailboats puffed with wind
and, all the while, that expansive vista,
in a dexterous triumph of perspective,
ushering my gaze—as if arm in arm
on an after-dinner stroll along the corso—
across the imperturbable piazza
to a harbor on an estuary or bay.
It can't be open sea, since tiny peaks,
barely evident, mark out the distance
gray-blue between gray water and blue sky.

There's no way of knowing if the ships at dock
are just now leaving or just returned,
as if to emphasize the movement back
and forth, the precious interconnection

and newly recognized but still untracked
proximity of an unfathomed world

and though we know—or think we know—the ship
on the water is headed into port
(the direction of the bulging in its sail)
we have no idea if it's visiting
or coming home—perhaps with a cargo
of fabrics, spices, perfumed oils, gems,
or fugitives, foreign ambassadors
armed with treaties, offers of marriage,
or unsuspected specimens of birds
snatched from a just now accessed longitude
and brought in recompense for unfound gold.

But—is it because of where I am?—that
pressure toward expansion seems ominous—
my Renaissance fabulists caught off guard
by the volatility of an idea
in transit, how quickly it's distorted,
apt to shatter, warp or decompose,
even secured in tempera on wood
susceptible to misapprehension.

Just look at me, willfully ignoring
the most likely meaning of these ships,
exploration almost never an end
in itself, but a noble-seeming guise
for acquisition, those tiny vessels
probably a subtle call to arms, their
openhanded patron, before a duke
(upon his half-brother's unsolved murder),
Italy's most brilliant *condottiere*
who lost an eye, but never a battle
waged in service to the highest bidder.
At times, he'd switch allegiance midway through.

———

Still, Urbino's citizens adored him,
Castiglione called him *the light of Italy,*
the masterpieces he commissioned—
his library, his twin-turreted palace,
Piero's portraits, the three *vedute*—
still among Europe's greatest wonders.

And here's a choice one, hanging in Berlin,
the single ideal city pressing out
into the world with what—for all its calm—
may well be a nefarious agenda.
Those ships, however tiny, alter everything,
arriving, leaving, waiting in the harbor,
or preparing for conquest, as seems all
too probable in this unquiet city,
the gash in its heart—near the Tiergarten,
the Brandenburg Gate—a self-inflicted
wound of a memorial—one more
contortion in an unsuccessful bid
for the insufficient solace of contrition.

But Berlin also teems with so much life,
half its citizens on bicycles,
the other half strolling in the parks,
the streets, the shops, the market stalls, the squares,
the river and canal banks overhung
with oak and linden, horse chestnut, birch
and so many bold, ecstatic buildings
(some undamaged, some reconstructed)—
Jugendstil, Bauhaus, New Objectivity—
a few perfecting their reflections in
a river or canal, like the sleek, white
Shell-Haus, with its billowing façade,
stone and glass made supple, their edges lulled
to undulate in fluid, clockwork waves:
Navy Headquarters for the Third Reich.

———

Everything was *something* for the Third Reich.
Just read the placards on the Wilhelmstrasse:
internal affairs, foreign affairs, Gestapo;
there are even photographs: department heads,
Obersturmführers, commissioners
and—close by, in the Potsdamer Platz
near the crowded entrance to the S-Bahn:
the Einsatzgruppen at the Eastern Front
(where my grandparents had left their siblings)
shooting whole families into ditches.
These photos, according to the caption,
were serving to familiarize Berlin
with the Nazis' *lesser-known* atrocities—
but why, then, the English translation?

Maybe it was meant for people like me,
to help us make it through the patched-up streets
of this preternaturally living city,
perhaps even accept its tainted offerings,
the limpid *veduta* for example,
or chamber concerts, recitals, operas,
their music so exquisitely refined
I'm half dissolved in it, half, briefly, found,
overwhelmed, consumed by sudden tears,
whose origin might be the sounds themselves
or might be their unfaltering inflection,
at least to my peculiarly tuned ear
each after-echo a reverberation
of the mute memorial in some nearby
train track, piece of brickwork, asphalt, stone,

a sonic mirror—if such a thing exists—
of the gaping havoc inside of me,
those images first witnessed far too young
and multiplied by what's too vast to see
except as blank triumvirates of zeroes,

as if any child or, even, adult
could navigate such decimated space,
assimilate such aggregates of losses

and here is a city clearly staggering
beneath their weight, offering to bear them
all instead of me . . .

          and, even if I'm
not quite able to accept, I take
comfort in my unexpected ally,
its every source of information
a mea culpa for another Jew.
On a label in the Pergamon: Ernst
Herzfeld, who excavated Samarra,
forced out *because of Jewish origins;*
on the placard by the steles, carved
with names of honored athletes, flanking
Hitler's Olympic stadium: special
mention of Adolf and Felix Flatow,
gold medalists in 1896,
who later perished in Terezhen ghetto

or the walls of text in a dining room
(a lovely lakeside villa in Wannsee):
mini-biographies of fifteen men
some of whom would live into their eighties—
who gathered there at noon, January
twentieth, 1942,
with maps and outlines and encoded terms
special action special treatment to devise
a blueprint for the *final solution.*

The meeting's diamond anniversary—
do we use that phrase for the horrific?—
seems to have gone largely unnoticed,

the world preoccupied with swearing in
a president of the United States
seventy-five years later to the minute,

about as portentous a conjunction
as I've ever encountered, history
on a collision course with our unhinged
already imploding present moment,
as if a standoff among the planets
had sapped gravity's remaining stamina
and loosed a free-for-all among the stars,

not that we require another sign
to know that things have gone awry
in what was meant to be *our* ideal city,
despite the most exquisitely laid plans,
by which I mean the US Constitution
tainted though it was (the three-fifths clause)
and still at the mercy of its readers,
not always primed to sort out truth from lies.

Or—as I heard argued on the radio—
the system don't operate itself, it's
people. The speaker, Omar Saunders, cleared
of murder after serving thirteen years,
ranked our jurisprudence (he'd studied law
in prison) with *the greatest in the world* . . .
these United States, in his regard,
a beautiful democratic republic

and if he thinks so, perhaps they could be.
But we'd have to tell ourselves a different
story, stop describing each infraction
in our long succession as a much
to be regretted aberration, when
in fact, it's what we do, have always done.

Perhaps if we'd owned up, built a few
disfiguring memorials, bemoaned
or at least allowed ourselves to see
our skulking points of likeness to Berlin,
its negative example might have spared us
this losing gamble on former greatness,
illusory at best, at worst disastrous—
but somehow the perennial go-to
cure-all for an empire in decline
or last-ditch detour before its fall.

Is that what's happening here? Our fall?
There are—read Gibbon—clear parallels to Rome,
but I really thought we had more time.
Still, how would I know? traipsing around
from ideal city to ideal city,
inventing more than one along the way,
Baltimore, for example, a disaster
by any reasonable calculus,
despite my saviors in the laundromat,
among them surely—I saw the clothing
they were folding—at least a few mothers
of sons, any of whom might, right now, be
lurching unsecured in a police van,
jostling an unprotected spine.

And what's my instinct? To get out of here,
to urge my daughters to start digging up
their grandfather's birth records in Europe,
though things seem to be worsening there too.
Perhaps an English teaching job in Guangzhou?
Ulan Bator? Kyoto? Kathmandu?
Still, they have no desire to leave and (I'm
proud of this of course) join all the protests,
women's marches, rallies for immigrants,
impromptu training sessions in resistance . . .

But me? I'd find some out-of-the-way
Renaissance courtyard in Urbino,
architectonically, at least, ideal
or better still, try to secure a berth
on the first of the tiny, perfectly
appointed ships (a sleek new caravel,
designed for ease of handling at high speeds,
conveyance of Columbus and Da Gama)
to shed its moorings at the water's edge,
where viewers' eyes infallibly converge
through the loggia's columns, past the piazza
in my lost-and-found panel in Berlin,
and make its way across the harbor,
around the estuary or the bay
to head out, full sail, on open ocean,
nothing in its sights but clouds or sun,
a seabird, perhaps, perhaps a dolphin,
a nightly deluge of stars and moon,
the bulges in its sails from steady wind
wafting me as far away as possible
to whichever invisible port of call
might be persuaded to take me in.

Stumble Stone

She tells the story every time we meet,
though she's not otherwise repetitious,
despite her age. (Erika turns eighty-eight

on her next birthday.) She gives sound advice,
as one of my few connections in Berlin,
where her mother grew up in the next-door house

to my friend Carol's father, and later on,
worked as his secretary. After the war,
they corresponded, visited: New York, Berlin.

The story takes place during the war:
Erika was with her mother on an errand,
ten years old and largely unaware

of wartime strictures—*I didn't understand*—
and there, in front of them, on the street,
was Carol's grandmother: *our dear, dear friend;*

it had been so long since we'd met;
to see her standing there, I was so happy
Erika ran to her, her arms out

she was like a grandmother to me
and the older woman pushed her away
saying *you don't see me you don't know me,*

protecting the child, presumably.
(Encounters with Jews were forbidden.)
She was deported soon after. (Her son

had left, with wife and child, in thirty-nine.)
Franziska Maass, by the way, was her name.
I only learned it from the stumble stone,

hidden by rain-soaked leaves the day I came.
I asked a woman leaving a house nearby;
she found it, cleared it off, made it gleam:

Franziska Maass, Geboren Moses 1880
Deportiert 14. 12. 1942
Ermordert in Auschwitz (no year, no day).

It was bronze, small, still fairly new.
Carol had come over for the ceremony
(affecting, but quick; it seems, they do

quite a few of them in a single day)
along with her sister, her sister's daughter.
Erika too, *like one of the family.*

Indeed, that's how Carol had described her.
And she proved a godsend. Erika's a marvel—
sharp, self-possessed, and, if quite proper,

so very welcoming on my arrival.
I visit her apartment; she comes to mine,
up for anything, happy to travel

across Berlin on public transportation.
A true pleasure every time we meet
and always, before long, our conversation

arrives at that moment on the street,
her thrilled sighting of her *dear dear friend,*
how she's running with her arms flung out—

her face tenses for the coming wound—
and how, once again, she's pushed away.
I was ten years old I didn't understand.

Our last meeting is on a rare, fine day:
we stroll by the canal near her house
for quite a while—Erika's spry—

until we find ourselves in semi-darkness
(in Berlin, in December, night comes early).
In no hurry to part—I fly off in a few days—

we decide to stop and have a coffee,
sit down—the only ones in the café.
Our drinks arrive and she begins her story:

an errand with her mother; *so happy*
to see her old friend walking on the street;
she was like a grandmother to me

she's running now; she has her arms flung out;
now she's rebuffed. *I couldn't understand.*
But her face looks less hurt than resolute.

This time her story doesn't end.
This time they're making an appointment.
She's no longer on familiar ground.

I can't follow her. What appointment?
Erika and her mother—how did we get here?—
are standing in Frau Maass's apartment

that very same evening. The rest is blur.
It's only Erika's question I remember
repeated over and over and over and over:

How could we hide her? She was our neighbor.
Everybody knew who she was.
Over and over: *How could we hide her?*

What's she telling me? I'm at a loss.
How could we hide her? She was our neighbor
It's hard to keep my eyes on Erika's face

and hard to look away *how could we hide her?*
I don't know how to hear what I'm hearing.
How could we hide her? She was our neighbor

What's she saying? What's even occurring?
I take nothing in, off balance, numb,
vaguely gearing up to be reassuring

but I don't think she ever gave me room
How could we hide her? Everyone . . .
one long beseeching continuum

punctured by a single revelation.
But what did she reveal? I'm still not certain.
Frau Maass might not have *asked* to be hidden;

maybe they'd come for some possession
to safeguard it for her—just one suitcase
allowed per person per deportation.

It's more than possible that's all it was,
the idea of *hiding* bitter hindsight—
the loop of regret after a loss

though it would explain that moment in the street
if Frau Maas was hoping they might hide her—
crucial, in public, to dissociate

(she'd smooth it over with the child later).
The more I try to think, the less is certain
starting—how did I miss this?—with the year

inscribed (I took a photo) on the stumble stone.
I find the file. Open it. The date:
Nineteen-forty-two. Twelve fourteen.

Clearly, if Erika was eighty-eight
in December 2016—she wasn't ten
but fourteen years old that day they met.

A child is so judgmental at fourteen,
so quick to blame, so full of certainties,
but powerless to put them into action.

How much better to have been oblivious,
cocooned inside a younger child's world.
Surely she would have suffered less

had she actually been a ten-year-old
as she was at the beginning of the war—
unless that's what she meant? *Ten years old*

in 1939, the first of September?
Ten years old when the war began?
It is, in fact, the way you remember

as you get older—a prolonged duration
telescoped to one outsize instant.
Perhaps for Erika that one rejection

or, rather, that one furtive appointment
was the defining moment of the war.
Who knows what that public rebuff meant?

Had Carol's grandmother asked them to hide her?
Could Erika's mother have turned her down
and still, after the war, found Carol's father?

Resumed her friendship with Franziska's son?
How could we hide her? She was our neighbor
In truth it's a legitimate question.

Everyone knew who she was. How could we hide her?
Odds are huge that they'd have been turned in.
Apparently, only about a quarter

of the Jews who were in hiding in Berlin
actually made it to the war's end.
Probably this scenario was common:

Rumors. Even the self-possessed frightened.
Disappearance after disappearance.
A last-ditch entreaty to a friend.

And, eventually, a city choked with penitents,
mostly gone by now, except for those
who were wartime children and adolescents,

each with his own story, her own loss.
Why not let it rest? She's an old woman.
And I don't know the facts. Not even close.

What is it I'm trying to write down?
Maybe it's that herculean persistence
in getting to the end (so that's the reason

for all those tellings!) her very last chance,
at least with me. Our final afternoon.
What is she after? Proof of innocence?

Or are these driven questions a confession?
She was fourteen. Of course, she's innocent.
Does she want compassion? Here's compassion.

I'm awash in it, drowning even, spent,
but it's overshadowed by paralysis,
a suspicion that I'm doubly deficient,

useless to my friend *and* traitorous
to the already many times betrayed.
And I'm powerless here. Forgiveness

is the province of the wronged; even God
can't offer it, unless the wronged refuse.
Three times, I think it is, then God will yield

or so—as Yom Kippur approached—they taught us
in Hebrew School year after year.
But why am I bringing up forgiveness?

Forgiveness has no application here;
she was fourteen years old. She's innocent.
And she's in real anguish. Her need is clear.

So why I am so tight-lipped, hesitant?
What's at stake here? Everyone's gone.
Why is it so hard to let a dormant

heart—six decades shut—crack open?
Why this terror of a tiny crack?
And why I am half hoping it will deepen

and, half, still desperate to shut it back?
At fourteen, a young girl suffers grief
and is still, at nearly ninety, heartsick.

———

Why not give her all I have to give?
What could she have done? She's innocent.
Why should she grieve and grieve and grieve?

She was fourteen years old, an adolescent.
Why deprive her? What could it achieve?
But I'm shut down, immobile, silent,

outwardly completely unresponsive,
her *How could we hide her* . . . like a holy chant
assigned by a confessor to relieve

the guilt of a despondent supplicant,
repetition itself the palliative.
Here's my prayer: that it be sufficient

or at least offer genuine reprieve,
that—the wronged long gone and God intransigent—
it won't matter that I can't forgive.

SS Photo, Auschwitz, 1944

Their backs are turned; we see no face,
unless you count the blurry one, in profile,
their children, too, just bundles, anonymous.

I'd no doubt find my double (shadowed eyes,
beak nose, high forehead, too gummy smile),
if their backs weren't turned. We see no face,

just coats and headscarves. But for the chimneys,
these might be any women facing exile
with their children and bundles, anonymous.

Today's have deserts, oceans, mountains to cross;
they too find soldiers, guns; they too stumble
while we, our backs turned, don't quite face

our part in this. We're charmed; we stay in place
or—if we so choose—travel at will
with our children, bundles. But who's anonymous?

We have our own borders and deportees
and, probably, right now, our own official
pulling children from their parents. He's our face
even with his back turned, anonymous.

Psalm 137, Berlin

(Museum Island, December 2016)

A massive triumph. We have the record:
a team of *two hundred to two hundred and fifty*
unearthing blue fragments, shard on shard

(the glaze was meant to look like lapis lazuli,
with highlights in faux turquoise, bronze and gold),
fifteen years *summer and winter, daily,*

each piece catalogued, numbered, labeled
until five hundred thirty-six crates
were tightly packed into a steamer's hold,

and heading to Basra, down the Euphrates,
across two oceans, the Elbe, the Spree,
and, finally, Berlin, where keen initiates

in the newborn discipline of archeology
would toil fifteen more years on the puzzle.
For each fresh obstacle, they'd find a strategy,

devise an ancient kiln to match the tile,
ignore a war, its wake, coming catastrophe
before they'd summon, intact, colossal,

blue and dreaming, from the stunned debris,
the Ishtar Gate to ancient Babylon's
legendary garden-dripping city.

It's approached between a double frieze of lions
in a stately, life-sized processional
beyond which rows of aurochs and dragons

(the auroch: an extinct Eurasian bull;
the dragon: a four-legged agglomerate
of feline torso, serpent's head and tail,

two paws, two talons) safeguard a façade
of high-voltage, fluorescent indigo
like lightning striking an electric field

of ink-blue larkspur. An openwork window
in the Islamic Museum one flight up
offers the most dream-inducing view:

one unbroken, otherworldly sweep
for people to gaze upon and wonder.
But aren't I obliged to sit and weep?

My holy temple razed to ash and cinder
by the man who names himself in this inscription
(*I Nebuchadnezzar . . . adorned . . . with splendor*)

Jerusalem *a widow,* forgotten.
But how can I weep when it's so stunning,
so all-enveloping? I know what's written,

but my *right hand* never had much *cunning*
(I favor my left). As for *my tongue,*
so far it appears to be functioning

and no one's yet *required of* me *a song.*
This isn't Babylon; it's a museum,
the Ishtar Gate, despite a steady throng

of selfie sticks, not even the gem
of its breathtaking, larcenous collection.
Babylon's leveled, while Jerusalem

for better or worse, is hanging on,
though each quarter tells a different story.
I'm in the Pergamon Museum, Berlin,

the second decade of the twenty-first century,
Babylon reduced? restored? to artifact
and Greek, Akkadian, and Hebrew hearsay

whereas Berlin (*if I forget thee*) is still intact
despite the newer, nearer cataclysm
it went to such great measures to inflict

on one-time stragglers from Jerusalem
who'd somehow wandered this far afield,
many, by then, so very much at home

they barely remembered they'd been exiled.
Better to have *sat down and wept,*
Babylon's oppression, by contrast, mild—

or at least less elaborately developed,
though even a very primitive procedure
like the one Pharaoh devised in Egypt

(*every boy ye shall cast in the river*)
could perpetrate wholesale genocide,
which seems to haunt each treasure flaunted here

on Museum Island. Egypt's are displayed
in the Neues, next door, while, just upstairs
(Islamic Art), there's a splendid inlaid

ceiling from the Alhambra, the very palace
where Spain's rulers signed the Inquisition.
It's as if each thing of beauty bore the impress

of concentrated mass annihilation.
Not that any evidence was ever found
of Moses or the Hebrew slaves' oppression,

the Red Sea parting to reveal dry land,
then engulfing Pharaoh and all his forces.
Measure for measure. Drowned for drowned.

Far too shapely for history, Exodus.
As for Babylon, the weepers' descendants
would prosper greatly, multiply, increase,

until, newly declared non-citizens
after two thousand five hundred years,
they flocked to Israel and independence.

There, in makeshift huts, they sat in tears
or so says my friend—born to two of them—
who describes, mortified (for their sake? hers?)

the barebones shack without a bathroom
in which she lived till she was six years old.
Still, given Iraq's future, given Saddam,

they were lucky to have been expelled.
But Saddam, too, had a long memory.
Preferring stone to words, he rebuilt

on the site of Nebuchadnezzar's fabled city
the ancient complex, complete with gate.
(Clearly our insatiability

for past glory is nearly infinite,
topped only by our craving for destruction.)
Saddam's artists copied this very gate,

which he couldn't get the Germans to return.
In all truth, it *doesn't* belong here,
though recent events—look at Bamiyan,

Palmyra—would suggest it's more secure.
So weirdly vengeful, to blow up a ruin,
the usual process easier to bear:

at first, years of disuse, dereliction;
the wooden parts dissolving into air,
then theft of the still useful brick and stone,

while flights of fancy from the exterior
are left to languish, then disappear
under earth and dust, layer upon layer,

buried until some restless, dauntless stranger
crossed a sea in search of vanished grace
or, turning up his fields, a local farmer

found a glint of blue and became curious.
Better to concentrate on people,
forget Palmyra, think Damascus.

In this, Berlin has worked hard to excel,
the rare advantage of an ugly legacy
a single-minded craving for good will,

which I encountered at a jam-packed Tuesday
lunchtime concert, Philharmonic Hall
(they're held weekly, in the foyer, free).

On chairs: elderly Germans, upright, formal,
young Syrians squatting on the floor,
exuberant at the traditional

instruments—the qanun I'd never seen before
with oud and lap drum and plangent voice
imposing on the unaccustomed air

a brief oasis of joyful noise.
A social worker introduced the band,
who'd met at the absorption center, refugees,

and thrown together a makeshift homeland
in their otherwise dissonant exile,
singing one's *song in a strange land*

for once not entirely impossible.
But things would change within a single week—
or so I imagine—for all these people

when a rented, explosive-laden truck
rammed into a Christmas marketplace,
bringing, along with pain and death and havoc,

undisguised suspicion and unease,
no doubt—at least in part—the bomber's aim,
so much easier to radicalize

a group of people who don't feel welcome.
My ninety days up, I meanwhile
readied myself to go back home

to a country newly unrecognizable
or—let's be accurate—newly unveiled,
beset by hate crimes, even at the small

Jewish cemetery in the aging neighborhood
of the stock fifties' semi-detached house
I first entered at a few days old,

where my parents lived into their eighties,
my life the very inverse of migration,
though my father was born where Belarus

meets southwestern Russia and the Ukraine,
a smallish vanished shtetl called Surazh.
By ten months old, he'd crossed an ocean

and always claimed long memories of haze,
of looking out on nothing. Open sea?
Did they even have windows in steerage?

My mother's parents made the same journey,
one, a toddler, one, fourteen years old,
all on her own. To cousins. She ran away

to sweatshops, night school, the Lower East Side.
They weren't comfortable, but they arrived—
had food to eat, didn't have to crowd

onto a much too small and leaky raft.
No refugee camp. No wire fence. No tent.
On the other hand, the world they left

they left forever—first, far too distant
to think of going back to; later on
but for its cemeteries, nonexistent

and even those (all that well-hewn stone,
there for the taking, put to other use)
not always very easy to track down,

which (I'm like a delayed-action compass:
sooner or later, one same direction)
brings us back—however circuitous

———

and rambling our progress—to Berlin—
which, for all its positive momentum,
still retains its pall of devastation.

But if we manage to hold onto equilibrium
despite exploding trucks, a melting arctic,
marauding asteroids, the neutron bomb,

Berlin, too, will be reduced to relic
(dug up by robots, probably, and scanned,
printed and rebuilt by a technique

still to be discovered or envisioned,
a brain implant, perhaps, its mechanism)
in a museum not even on solid ground

but air or ocean, on another solar system,
the earth—how could it not?—of course succumbing
to one despoiler or other, some cataclysm

only birds and animals see coming.
Forgive me; once you start such speculation
(the recourse of the lost) it's all-consuming

and who can prove me wrong? Still, fascination
with our obsolescent bits and pieces
seems dubious, as does continuation

of so willfully profligate a species.
We have enough stuff in museums as it is,
should find more compelling enterprises,

for example—imagine!—some lasting space
for the droves and droves of people on the move
or, if that's impossible, perhaps a pulse

for each otherwise unresponsive
one-time dreamer fished out of the sea
or, if that fails, as least someone who'll grieve,

however insufficiently and briefly.
Maybe it's time to sing a different psalm.
Those who sow in tears shall reap in joy.

(126) *We were like them that dream*
Not a psalm of exile, but return
But some have wept for a millennium.

Surely, by now, joy should have kicked in.
Though who am I kidding? one person's dream
involves another person's devastation.

That too—I've stifled it—is in my psalm.
And take this gate, this city, ancient Babylon.
Begin with its frame: each wooden beam

had to be transported, heaved, cut down—
slave labor, no doubt, relentless hardship—
and that's before we factor in the stone

to be chiseled, quarried, hoisted up
(the broad walkway was paved in limestone),
the clay to gather, mix with straw, then shape,

bake and paint and glaze and glaze again,
the molds to design for each particular
(a dragon's tail, forked tongue, eagle talon,

an auroch's horn, a lion's mouth, mid-roar,
his tensed flanks poised to take a step).
And this just a single gate, for Ishtar,

———

to just one city on a sprawling map,
one epoch in a harrowing continuum,
the one trove of shards we've managed to keep.

Meanwhile, some of my captives from Jerusalem—
I checked the dates; they overlap:
twelve years between the sacking of Jerusalem

and this gate's completion—might have helped shape
a laggard bull or two, or dragon or lion,
that is, if one can learn such craftsmanship

in a dozen years. More likely, they coaxed stone
from a tightfisted quarry, hauled it up,
dragged it to the site, fighting starvation,

typhus, dysentery, lack of sleep.
Or am I confusing Babylon and Sachsenhausen
(some twenty miles from here—an easy trip,

from Friedrichstrasse, on the S-Bahn
to Oranienburg—the final stop
and then a fifteen-minute walk through town)?

Clearly, it's time I too hung up my harp
with its one obsessive note; I'll use a linden
if there's no willow. Maybe I can help

some sufferer with wounds still open,
still revocable, however deep,
and likely, given the look of things, to deepen,

start small, perhaps, a phone call, envelope
or at least get out of this museum
into broad daylight, take the leap

———

into my own, perhaps still salvageable, time,
or, if not a leap, a baby step.
There's at least a chance, however slim,

of blunting some fraction of the hardship
to which I've given far too little attention.
But first, I have to get some kind of grip,

focus, mobilize, let myself in
for a roller-coaster apprenticeship
in the fundamentals of frustration

(hope then letdown, letdown then hope).
I'm ill-adapted, but if not now, when?
And where, exactly? I doubt my map

will offer a definitive direction.
But, just in case, let me open it up,
get my bearings, find the nearest U-Bahn,

catch my breath a minute, maybe stop
with this knot of tourists (for once there's sun)
lolling by the water, on this step,

comparing notes in Spanish, French, Italian,
Dutch, Chinese . . . One couple's getting up
so now there's room. Let me sit down

and give my thoughts a minute to regroup.
Whatever they conjure up will keep.
Just for a minute. Let me just sit down—
there's even a river here—and weep.

CPSIA information can be obtained
at www.ICGtesting.com
Printed in the USA
LVHW030625100223
739115LV00004B/443